K-3

D1318761

PENN HILLS LIBRARY
240 ASTER STREET
PITTSBURGH, PA 15235

In Spring

by Jane Belk Moncure
illustrated by
Marie Claude Monchaux

APR 1995

E
J
81154
MON

PENN HILLS LIBRARY

THE
CHILD'S
WORLD

ELGIN, ILLINOIS 60120

Distributed by Childrens Press, 1224 West Van Buren Street,
Chicago, Illinois 60607.

Library of Congress Cataloging in Publication Data

Moncure, Jane Belk.
   Spring.

   Summary: Fourteen poems celebrate the flowers,
singing birds, baby ducks, and other signs that
spring has arrived.
   1. Spring—Juvenile poetry.   2. Children's
poetry, American.   [1. Spring-Poetry.   2. American
poetry]   I. Monchaux, Marie Claude, ill.   II. Title.
PS3563.O517S6   1985   811'.54   85-11672
ISBN 0-89565-327-3

© 1985 The Child's World and Abdo Consulting Group, Inc.
All rights reserved. Printed in U.S.A.

3 4 5 6 7 8 9 10 11 12 R 91 90 89

In Spring

It's that windy,
   kite-flying
   time of the year
when the robins'
   "Cheep . . . cheep"
says, "SPRING IS HERE!"

Wake~Up Time

It's wake-up time for flowers.
I find them every year,
    growing in the sunshine,
    knowing spring is here.
How do they know
    it's time to grow?
They have a way to tell.
You can too.
Here's what to do.
Just close your eyes
    and smell!

In the Park

It's spring in the park.
How do I know?
I see baby ducklings,
    all in a row.
They're swimming,
    quack-quacking,
    and diving for snails.
First I see heads.
Then I see tails!

The Robins' Secret

I know a secret
   I can't tell.
The robins hid their nest
   so well, but . . .
   one day I climbed
   the apple tree;
   and I found it,
   accidentally!
There were four blue eggs.
Oh, please don't tell.
The robins hid their nest
   so well!

In the Meadow

It's springtime in the meadow;
   the grass grows tall and wild.
And mother rabbit watches
   each baby rabbit child
   play hide and seek
   and rabbit tag.
Then, when the day is over,
   they go to sleep in
   rabbit beds of buttercups
   and clover.

Dress~Up Time

All winter long
   the trees are bare.
But when springtime comes,
   look what they wear:
   blossoms of lavender,
   purple and pink.
Trees like to dress up
   for springtime,
   I think!

In the Pond

How does a bull frog
    know it's spring?
He blinks his eyes
    and begins to sing.
Frog music is different
    from yours and mine.
But to froggie ears,
    "Rib-it, rib-it"
    sounds fine.

Hi, Wind

"Hi, wind," I say.
"I know you're there . . .
   pulling my kite
   into the air.
"I cannot see you,
   but I know
   when you come
   and when you go."

The Easter Bunny

Wouldn't it be a funny thing
   if the Easter bunny slept
   through spring?
"It would never happen,"
   Daddy said. "For the Easter
   bunny hops out of bed
   the minute the first baby
   robin peeps.
"Then the Easter bunny never
   sleeps until after his
   baskets are stuffed with treats,
   such as colored eggs
   and chocolate sweets."

19

A Rainy Day

It's a wonderful day
   for turtles
   and fish and polliwogs;
   for flowers and grass
   and ducklings;
   for toads and jumpy frogs.
It's a wonderful day
   for gardens,
   and for the cherry tree.
But it's a drippety-droppety,
   mud puddle-hoppety,
   umbrella day for me.

My Garden

Come and see my garden.
Come and watch it grow.
The carrot seeds I planted,
   a week or two ago,
   have feathery green leaves
   above the ground
   and orange roots
   down below.

Flower Friends

I have friends.
Do flowers have friends?
Look closely
   and you'll see.
A butterfly
   is a flower's friend.
So is a honeybee.

25

Daydreaming

I wonder how the flowers know . . .
   it's time to bloom?
Who tells them so?
They cannot hear or see a thing
   and yet they start to grow
      in spring.
I wonder who tells
   the willow trees,
      the ducks, the lilies,
         the honeybees?
In spring things grow
   so fresh and new.
I wonder . . . am I growing too?

Mother's Day

Guess what I did on Mother's Day?
I hid little notes everywhere —
   in the refrigerator,
   underneath mom's chair,
   in her sewing basket,
   her pocketbook,
   her coat.
I put a special message
   on every single note.
I wrote in big red letters,
   "I LOVE YOU, MOM, I DO."
And when she found my notes,
   she said, "I love you special too."

It's Spring

No more snowsuits.
No more caps.
No more boots
   or winter wraps.
No more, "Wear your
   mittens, dear."
It's spring,
   and barefoot time
   is near!